meditation
is *easy*

meditation
is *easy*

Greer Allica

Penguin Books

Penguin Books Australia Ltd
487 Maroondah Highway, PO Box 257
Ringwood, Victoria 3134, Australia
Penguin Books Ltd
Harmondsworth, Middlesex, England
Penguin Putnam Inc.
375 Hudson Street, New York, New York 10014, USA
Penguin Books Canada Limited
10 Alcorn Avenue, Toronto, Ontario, Canada M4V 3B2
Penguin Books (NZ) Ltd
Cnr Rosedale and Airborne Roads, Albany, Auckland, New Zealand
Penguin Books (South Africa) (Pty) Ltd
5 Watkins Street, Denver Ext 4, 2094, South Africa
Penguin Books India (P) Ltd
11, Community Centre, Panchsheel Park, New Delhi 110 017, India

First published by Penguin Books Australia Ltd 1998

15 14 13 12 11 10 9 8 7

Designed by Anitra Blackford, Penguin Design Studio
Typeset in 11/16 pt New Baskerville by Post Pre-press Group, Brisbane
Printed in Australia by Australian Print Group, Maryborough, Victoria

National Library of Australia
Cataloguing-in-Publication data:

Allica, Greer, 1944– .
    Meditation is easy.

    ISBN 0 14 027892 3.

    1. Meditation. I. Title.

158.12

www.penguin.com.au

I dedicate this book to my mother,
whose love and belief in my
ability have been steadfast

Dear Reader,

I came to meditation for probably the same reason that you've picked up this book. I wasn't happy. I wasn't coping. All the situations in my life seemed designed to challenge me and put me off balance. There *had* to be a better way to live.

Meditation gave me a way out. I persisted with it because I needed it. I wanted to do more than just survive. Surely, there could be more love, more joy and celebration. Meditation helped me find these life-giving qualities and led me down a path of self-discovery.

Your need may not be as urgent as mine, but if you are prepared to give meditation a go, I know that you will be rewarded.

This book is like a kaleidoscope showing you the different pieces of a pattern. You can open the book anywhere and you'll get a small picture of what meditation is all about, but if you read the *whole* book the total pattern will fall into place. Each double page is like a jewel – there is information that is solid and substantial and there is something to take you further, to nourish and sustain you. There is both mind food and soul food.

Read the book with a light heart. Make it fun. Make it pleasurable . . . and easy. It took me a long, long time to realise that I could actually choose whether to dance through life or to struggle. You too can choose.

Happy reading . . . and meditating!

Greer Allica

Meditation is . . . *easy!*

Meditation is as simple as breathing

After you've practised it for a while
you'll find that you are *living* meditation,
effortlessly, not *doing* it. But in order to
make this leap, you must prepare yourself
by taking the first small steps, like a child
learning to walk. Think only about
each step.

Follow the breath

Take a deep breath in and out. Follow it with your mind. Focus only on the breath, nothing else. You can breathe *and* notice the breath at the same time.

Meditation is a bridge . . .

. . . between the inner and the outer self; the physical, mental, emotional, spiritual self. The more connections you make between your inner and outer world the more integrated you will become.

Sens(e)itive exploring

Start with the physical. Explore the five senses: hearing, seeing, taste, touch and smell. Reach the *inner* sense through remembering and imagination. For example: look at a flower, then shut your eyes and hold the picture in your mind. If you lose the picture, look again.

Meditation needs a relaxed body

If you are not relaxed, your body is a distraction. Relaxing the body prepares you for the deeper experience of meditation.

Body sensing

Sit or lie quietly with your eyes closed and
listen to your body. Let your mind pass
through every part of the body from the
head to the toes. Concentrate and feel
the tension. Exaggerate the tension.
Release the tension. Feel the difference.

Meditation is mindfulness

You are in charge of your mind; it doesn't control you. Begin to monitor *what* you are thinking. Own your thoughts and know that you can change them. You can choose to have positive, uplifting thoughts or negative, judgemental thoughts.

Self-talk

Write down ten things you like about yourself and ten things that you dislike. Which list was easier to write? With what thoughts are you feeding your life? Where did they come from? How do they limit you?

Meditation is letting go . . .

. . . of the tension in your body, of the feelings that cause the tension, of the thoughts that limit you. Be open to who you are. First acknowledge what you feel. Be an explorer and listen to what is *behind* the feeling. Never deny your feelings.

Pinpointing

Take time when you are feeling depressed
to acknowledge the depression, rather
than suppress it. Find where the
depression is centred in your body and
stay focused there. Listen to what your
feeling is telling you. Don't rationalise
it away.

Meditation gives you energy

When you feel centred from meditating,
rather than scattered and over-stimulated,
you'll find an abundance of energy. You'll
learn to focus on what is important in
your life and release the rest.

Light body

Imagine your body filled with light.
Breathe it into every cell. See, feel and
direct the light. Imagine that every cell is
being renewed, revitalised, made healthy
and whole. When the entire body is filled
with light, visualise it radiating from the
body as far as your inner eye can see.

Meditation brings awareness

Be responsible for who you are and what you become. You are not just a body. You have feelings, thoughts and a spirit, and they are all related. Nothing operates in a vacuum. The more you meditate, the less you will blame people or events for things that are truly your responsibility.

Is it me or is it you?

In a still, quiet space, breathe deeply,
and explore a situation where you are
in conflict. Look beneath your feelings.
What are you defending? What are
your fears? What's in it for you?

Meditation helps you distinguish . . .

. . . between illusion and reality, between the person you want others to believe you are and the person you really are.

Who am I?

Breathe deeply till you are quiet and relaxed, then ask the question: 'Who am I?' Every time you get an answer, ask the question again. Then visualise yourself in a mirror and ask: 'Who are you?' Where are the differences?

Meditation dissolves the masks . . .

. . . you put on to hide your fears and your doubts. But don't be afraid. *You* are in charge of taking off the masks when they no longer protect you.

The soldier

Imagine that you are a soldier, come
home from a battle. In the privacy of your
bedroom, take off the layers of your
armour. As you place each piece of
armour on the bed, look at it closely.
What does it represent? Name it.

Meditation changes brainwaves

In your normal waking state, your
brainwave frequency varies from 14 to
30 cycles per second. This is called Beta.
During meditation you reach the Alpha
state, and the frequency is lower – from
7 to 14 cycles per second.

From Beta to Alpha

Exercise, relax, let go and slow the mind.
Later, you reach beyond thought. Find a
moving object: a tree in the wind, or a
candle flame. Observe it, then remember
it and shut your eyes. Open them when
the image fades. Repeat the steps.

Meditation is stillness

Once you can meditate, you'll find the
still, calm pool in the midst of turmoil.
You won't have to remove yourself from
the situation. The turmoil will be like
ripples in your pool – passing.

Pool of reflection

Imagine a pool of still, clear water. See
the light shining through to the sandy
bottom. Surround your pool with
beautiful trees and plants. Visualise it
often till it is imprinted in your mind.
Come back to the still mind-pool
whenever you need.

Meditation is a journey

Meditation takes you places. The scenery is constantly changing. It is exciting because the journey is full of surprises – unexpected twists and turns in the road.

Once you have set out, you won't want to stop. All that is required is persistence and a spirit of adventure.

Life path

Imagine yourself at the beginning of a road. This is where you are now. You are carrying your most prized possessions on your back. Look at the signpost – this is where you are going.

Travel the road as far as you can, noting everything you see along the way. Perhaps you meet other people. What part of you do they represent?

Meditation transcends time

Time is linear. When you meditate, your experience of time is different. You can span years and centuries and jump between them; you can encompass other realities in a meditation experience.

Time leap

Step into your future – a year from now,
five years, ten years. Who are the people
around you? Where are you? What are
you doing?

Review your life now in the light of
what you have discovered.

Meditate on the 'now'

The more you practise meditation,
the more fully you will experience
each moment. You will be entirely
in the present, without distraction.

The considered walk

In some Zen Buddhist retreats, the devotees spend hours walking backwards and forwards in deliberately slow motion as they meditate on the rise and fall of each foot and its deliberate placing on the path.

Spend 10 minutes of total concentration on your footfall.

Meditation and concentration are cousins

Concentration is an important stepping stone to meditation. Concentration enables you to focus on the particular. Meditation allows you to see the whole.

A rose is a rose is a rose

Take a single-stemmed, perfumed rose.
Examine it, using all five senses.
Concentrate till you begin to lose the
boundaries between yourself and the
rose. Now you are really meditating!

If your mind wanders, bring it back
to the rose.

Meditation has many paths

There is no single way to meditate. You must find the way that suits you – the easiest way. Perhaps your way will be through breathing, through silence and non-thought, through visualisation, or through chanting.

Explore

Don't be afraid to experiment and to explore. After several years of meditation, you'll probably find that the way you began to meditate isn't the way you do it now. When you become more proficient, you'll find easier, more straightforward paths to the meditative state.

Meditation aids creativity

Much research has been done on the links between meditation and creativity. Because meditation links the conscious with the subconscious, the mind has greater access to the imagination, to dreams and reflections.

Soul picture

Have paints and paper ready. Now play
some mood music. Shut your eyes;
breathe slowly and deeply till you are
relaxed. Open your eyes and begin
to paint using colour, shape and pattern
to express your soul's essence. Don't try
to paint anything representational.

How did you feel about the experience and what did it reveal to you?

Meditation brings integration

The perceptive, intuitive, encompassing
right brain functions together with the
rational, analytical, dissecting left brain.
Meditation balances and centres so that
neither brain hemisphere dominates.

Figuring

Shut your eyes and imagine that you
are connecting the right and left
hemispheres of your brain. With your
mind's eye draw a figure eight lying on
its side. Draw the eight bigger and bigger
till it fills your whole mind screen, then
trace the eight back the other way.

Meditation has physical benefits

Meditation lowers blood pressure, slows the heartbeat and brainwave patterns, decreases oxygen consumption and carbon dioxide elimination, reduces the amount of lactic acid in the body, and improves circulation.

Progressive relaxation

Relax the body with the aid of the mind
and the breath. Progress from head to
throat, shoulders, arms, hands, spine,
heart, ribs, lungs, stomach, intestines,
hips, legs, feet and, lastly, toes. Return to
any parts of the body that are still tense.

Meditate in the midst of chaos

After all, this is the purpose of meditation! An untrained body will become tense in stressful circumstances. An untrained mind will dwell on the current problem. Emotions that aren't under control either engulf or explode. Integrate the body, mind and emotions.

Three simple steps

Chaotic situations don't allow for
elaborate routines.

1. Breathe into and out from the solar
   plexus.
2. Mentally repeat, 'This too will pass',
   as you release your breath.
3. Don't let your mind wander from
   this central thought till the worst
   has passed.

If you can do all of this in natural
surroundings, so much the better.

Meditation is being,
not mastery

Mastery involves striving and effort.
It is goal-centred. Meditation requires
openness, listening and letting go.
It is soul-centred.

Clouds passing

Sit outside and simply observe clouds
passing through the blue sky. Now shut
your eyes and observe your thoughts in
the same way, as they pass like clouds
through your consciousness and out of
your mind screen. Don't analyse or hold
on to your thoughts.

Meditate on your dreams

Your dreams are your highest vision.
Decide what is important in your life,
then explore and define your dream so
that it can materialise.

Discover the obstacles and face them
one at a time.

Star

Make a link of intention between yourself
and your dream. Visualise a shining star,
far off in the heavens. Beams of light
extend from the star to you.

Now send your vision on the beams of
light to the centre of the star and see its
energy radiating back.

Meditate on your star every day.

Meditation requires commitment

Don't try meditation today and forget it tomorrow. If you really want to change your life (because that is what meditation will do), give it everything you've got.

Forget about effort and expectations – they are heavy concepts and will weigh you down! Meditate with joy and a light heart.

Expect to have failures and to learn from them.

Contract

Encourage your commitment with a contract, which you sign and date. Write it on a beautiful sheet of coloured paper. Read it often.

'I [your name] fully and freely allow time for meditation each day of my life. I know that by doing this I will be a calmer and happier person, and this will benefit myself and all those around me.'

Meditation is the sound of silence

Like the sound of one hand clapping, the stiller you become, the more you hear. Listen, and you will become more sensitive to your inner being, and to the energy around you.

Contrast – the church and the station

Sit in an empty church and tune into the surrounding energy, then contrast this by sitting at a noisy railway station.

Shut your eyes and concentrate on the sounds till you reach the silence beyond.

Meditate on the beauty around you

You'll be surprised at the effects. It is uplifting and energising. It will reduce your stress.

Thinking beautiful thoughts creates more of them. It is positive and unifying.

The meadow

Create a scene in nature that is real or imagined, or both. It could be a meadow. Place yourself in it. Don't observe it. Visualise every detail, and use your inner senses to bring it alive.

Make it special – a place of refuge. Know that you can return to the meadow often.

Meditation is harmony

By meditating often you will be able to
bring the conflicting parts of yourself into
greater harmony. You will notice things
that you never saw, heard or felt before
and, consequently, you will feel more in
touch with the world around you.

From self to world

The conflict within yourself is but a
smaller version of the conflict within and
between other countries. As each of us
becomes more attuned, so too will the
world. Visualise the troubled spots of the
world and send light and love to them.

Meditation is not a task

Don't say: 'I'll *have* to meditate.' You'll
end up hating meditation – and feeling
guilty!

Remember – it's *your* choice.

About fun and joy

- Cultivate an attitude of anticipation – look forward to your quiet times.
- Develop a ritual. For example: light a candle or spread out a piece of silk material in front of you; find a mandala to hang on the wall in the room where you meditate.
- Discover the joy of movement through dance, tai chi or hatha yoga. Explore different ways of meditating.

Meditate any time

There's no rule that says you *must*
meditate at a certain time. You can't
predict when you will need meditation.
However, it is helpful while you are
learning to establish a routine, so
meditation can become a pattern in
your life. Morning and/or evening
are good times for meditating.

Sunrise and sunset

Give yourself a treat. Get up and watch the sunrise. Notice the difference in the air; watch the dark turn to light, and the brilliant colours as they fade. Shut your eyes and hold the sunrise in your mind. Feel it.

Do the same at sunset. (The beach is ideal for meditating on sunsets.)

Meditation is a well of strength . . .

. . . on which you can draw in stressful times. Reach into the well for what you need and you'll find ways to deal with the brick walls of your life.

The well represents the infinite wisdom within and around you.

The bottomless well

Visualise a well that never goes dry. Dip in your bucket whenever you need and see what comes up.

You can choose to send down an empty bucket on its rope, or put a question in the bucket.

Meditation is a world in a grain of sand

Each grain of sand is a small part of the whole, yet holds the essence of the whole.

In the same way, you are a small part of the whole, yet have the elements of wholeness within you.

Small is beautiful

Find a small natural object, perhaps
a rock or a piece of driftwood, and
minutely examine it using all your senses.
Then shut your eyes and feel the essence
of the object in your hands.

Meditation is a growth process

If you meditate regularly, your personal growth will accelerate. Change will be easier and you'll struggle less. You'll know when your belief structures no longer serve you, and you'll be willing to let them go.

Freewheeling

An activity to do after meditating: on a sheet of paper, write down one of your strongly held beliefs. Circle it and then, without thinking too much, connect the circle with statements, phrases or words that you associate with the belief.

What new insights have you gained?

Meditation empowers you

As you learn more deeply about yourself through meditation, you realise that you are responsible for your own happiness.

You stop being a victim of life's circumstances and do something about changing whatever '*dis*empowers' you. First you might have to change your attitude.

Where did it come from?

Look at a situation where you feel out
of control. What is behind your feeling?
Where is it located in your body? What
protective label have you given it (for
example, anger, resentment, hurt) so
that you don't have to delve any deeper?
What are the ideas behind the feeling
and where did *they* come from?

Meditation is openness

The more you meditate, the more self-aware you become. This means that you come face to face with your fears, and replace them with understanding, compassion and love.

When you open your heart, you no longer regard other people as a threat.

The waterlily

Find a waterlily and watch its progress
from closed bud to fully open flower.
Imagine yourself as a closed bud. The
petals open one by one to reveal the
centre of your flower. At the centre is a
core of pure light (your potential).

As you breathe in, draw in light.
Breathe out and see the light radiate
in every direction.

Meditation is wholeness

When the mind isn't fighting the emotions, when the conscious isn't in conflict with the subconscious, when the ego isn't masking the higher self, you can find your own wholeness.

Meditation will lead you out of all these conflicts; it is a simple and beautiful path.

I am complete and whole

Sit cross-legged or on a straight-backed
chair with your hands resting on your
lap, palms upward and your thumb and
forefinger touching. Turn inwards and
contemplate your own wholeness.
Breathe it in and mentally repeat:
'I am complete and whole.'

Meditation brings peace

The more you still the mind and quieten
the emotions, the more peace you will
find. Meditation aligns the body, mind
and emotions with the spirit so that they
operate in harmony, together.

Bringing it all together

Scan your body from head to toe and feel all tension dropping away. Imagine that conflicting thoughts and distractions are balloons. Let go the string of each one. Then get in touch with the associated feelings and release them too.

Feel a sense of lightness and peace.

Meditate without expectation

It's much more fun and it's easier too.
Having no expectations means not
judging yourself, not setting impossible
standards or impossible goals, not putting
yourself down or comparing yourself with
others. Give yourself a chance, by being
kind to yourself.

Yes it is, no it isn't

On a sheet of paper write down your
expectations about meditation, and
about yourself as a meditator, then on the
other side of the paper write a counter-
statement to each assertion. The thoughts
that feed your mind influence your
emotions and your behaviour. Look
at them.

Meditation becomes a habit

If you are motivated, if you've removed
your mind's stumbling blocks, if you're
willing to give it time, energy and
persistence, meditation becomes a habit
and not a chore. A habit that is adopted
for any length of time becomes familiar.
And natural. You won't need to 'do'
meditation any more; it will be a part
of you.

The right frame of mind

Think about your self-talk. Get rid
of the 'shoulds', and the 'ought tos'.
Reprogramme yourself so that you
see meditation as your best friend, as
something that will make you freer and
happier and actually *give* you *more*
time, when you are not caught up with
destructive and distracting thoughts
or feelings.

Meditation requires adaptability

The moment you start meditating, you're headed for change. It might sound frightening, but it's not, because *you* are in charge of your own pace. Go as slowly or as fast as you wish. Better this than circumstances dictating the change, which is a much more traumatic situation.

No change means rigidity; being in a straitjacket for your entire life is most uncomfortable!

In a corner

Think of a situation where you have dug
in your heels and forced yourself into a
corner.

Look at how *you* got there (not how
someone else pushed you into the
corner!). Examine your attitudes. Are you
in victim mode, and if you are, what can
you do to regain your own power in the
situation (and not over the other person)?

Meditation is healing

When meditation becomes part of your
life, it is a gentle, safe and deep healer.
You can go as far as you wish.

When you use meditation for healing
yourself and/or others, it becomes
'dynamic' – you are actively engaged
in making something happen.

The colour of pain

Heal yourself by isolating the pain. Shut
your eyes and take your consciousness to
the painful area. Find the centre (the
point at which the pain is most intense)
and define the boundaries.

Give the pain a colour and mentally
shift it out of your body. Remember to
release with the breath as well.

Meditation has a language

Like dreams, meditation deals in the language of symbols. The symbols are yours – you don't need to ask anyone else what they mean. They come from your *sub*conscious mind and offer valuable insights.

Logbook

Keep a logbook of your own personal
symbols from your dreams and your
meditations. You will find recurring
images. What do you associate with
these symbols? Meditate on them and
ask them why they have appeared.

It's not as funny as it seems!

Meditation needs patience

Understand that you are a student and that no accomplishment or piece of knowledge is instant. Nor is it complete. It takes time to see the whole picture. Be prepared for setbacks and feelings of discouragement.

Focus on the gains

Failure and success are no yardsticks
for meditation.

Every time a meditation works for you,
remember it and let this knowledge lead
you further. Use this positive thought as
a fallback for when you *can't* meditate.
There is always another time, another
chance.

Meditation has a tradition . . .

. . . in both the East and the West.
Christianity uses prayer and singing. Out
of Hinduism came yoga. Buddhist texts
describe the Eightfold Path, a meditative
practice to end suffering. Zen Buddhism
emphasises breathing and posture. Out of
Islam came Sufi mysticism and meditation
through dance and music. Judaism uses
symbols.

Find out about . . .

. . . Saint Ignatius de Loyola and
Gregorian chants; raja yoga and the
chakras of kundalini yoga. Discover the
paradoxes of Zen. What is the Qabbalah
and the Tree of Life, and who are the
Whirling Dervishes? Look at the Sufi
poetry of Rumi.

Meditation is mind-blowing

Meditation takes you places where you never thought of going. It constantly surprises and stretches your mind.

If you have phobias, you'll find out why.

When you are sick, meditation will help you discover the emotional, mental and spiritual causes of your sickness, and show you how to take responsibility for your own wellbeing.

Speed-writing surprises

Write three pages as fast as you can
(speed stops your internal censor)
about anything that comes into your
head. Then pick the part which seems
most important to you and meditate on it.
Select the key sentence and then the
key word from the writing. Where are
the links between your three choices?

Meditate on a mountain top . . .

. . . real or imagined! It's great for giving
you an overview of your life, seeing where
you have come from and where you are
going. It gives you a perspective on your
problems and helps you to aim more
realistically.

From child to adult

See yourself as a child once more at the foot of a mountain. What colour predominates? What is happening and how do you feel about it?

Ascend the mountain; the top is where you are now at this stage in your life. Look back at your path and its important milestones.

The bird overhead represents your potential. Name it.

Meditation is part of living

Don't think that you can slot meditation into a separate corner of your life and go on living the same way as you did before you meditated. It doesn't work like that!

If you want to use meditation when you most need it, make it a central part of your existence. You'll never regret it.

Why do I do it?

Look at your reasons for meditating. Are
you doing it because it's trendy, because
your friends meditate, because you think
you ought to, because you need to,
because you want to, because you
were advised to?

Can you meditate with joy and a sense
of excitement?

Can you be open to whatever might
come out of it?

Meditate alone or in a group

Learning with a group is encouraging and fun. Being part of a group means, though, that you go at the pace of the group, but you also benefit from other people's meditation experiences. A group meditation has a powerful energy.

If you want to learn to meditate on your own, you'll need more self-discipline.

There's no reason why you can't do both.

Decisions, decisions!

There are many good books (see if there's a 'Further Reading' section at the back of these books) available in libraries and bookshops.

Look in your local newspaper or a national newspaper for workshops and courses.

Ask your friends for information.

Inquire at tertiary colleges, adult education centres and community houses.

Meditate on your potential

You can't envisage your own potential until you have a sense of 'self' that you learn to value. Meditation will help you find your own meaning, and the ways to express your talents.

'If' and 'but' blocks

Don't put barriers in your path with qualifiers like 'if only' or 'but'. These words are disguises for something you're not facing up to. Look at what it is.

Allow your potential to unfold. Look first at the blocks, then visualise yourself as having *already* achieved what you want. Release your potential in a bubble of light. Move one step at a time.

Meditation leads to humility

It's humbling to see your own ego, full of pride and self-importance, wanting to save face, or to bully others into doing what you want.

It's easy to see this in others, but meditation will make you see it in yourself.

Self-questioning

Look at the ways you justify yourself.
When are you defensive with others?
What credit do you give to yourself that
is really due to others? How do you make
others conform to your wishes?

Meditation makes sense

What is the point of going at life helter-skelter when you don't know what you're doing or why you're doing it and why you never have a moment to spare in which to enjoy, to be, to reflect.

Meditation gives you the time out – time to disconnect from the everyday hassles and connect to the central thread of your life.

Time out

Look at your priorities. Are you on a
treadmill and afraid to get off? Are you
living consciously or unconsciously? Do
you put love and energy into all that you
do or are you feeling hunted, resentful,
dissatisfied?

If *you* can't make time for yourself,
no one else will.

Meditation is not a religion

Although meditation has long been a
part of the major religions, you don't
have to be religious in order to meditate.

Meditation has no dogma, though it
can have ritual. It is a way of being, rather
than a belief structure.

A way of being

What *is* the way you want to be at this point in your life? What is your meaning and purpose? Look at your short-term and long-term goals.

Visualise *your* way of being and surround yourself with pictures and words that reinforce your vision.

Meditate with a mantra

A mantra is a chant that you repeat over and over, either aloud or silently. It can be sung or spoken.

You can make up your own mantra or be given your own special one by a teacher.

Your mantra can be meaningful or made up of random sounds and syllables.

Some well-known mantras

- Om
- Om Namaha Shivaya
- God is Love
- Hare Krishna
- La ilaha illa Llah
- Om Mane Padme Hum
- Allah hu
- I am the Way, the Truth and the Light

Meditation and success

You can't expect to have instant success, or *always* be successful with meditation. People who have meditated for years still have times when it's difficult to meditate, and so will you.

Be kind to yourself and persevere. Don't set yourself up for failure. It's okay not to meditate – sometimes.

A creative approach

By having a creative attitude to meditation, you'll be more successful. When you *can't* meditate, use it as an occasion to understand *why* (turn the negative into a positive).

Vary your ways of meditating – experiment; make things up; adopt a new ritual. Draw, paint or write. Take a walk.

Don't take yourself too seriously!

Meditate on the wind

Develop your listening skills. Tune into something that has no form, so that you won't be distracted by the strong sense of seeing. The more you practise on the externals, the easier it is to hear your *inner* voice, or your higher self.

In and around and through

Sit on a cliff top on a windy day. Shut
your eyes and breathe in the wind; feel it
touch the surface of your body. Allow the
wind to penetrate and 'blow' inside you.
Feel its energy. Absorb the scents that the
wind carries.

Meditation is calming

Meditation quietens all the sensations
felt in the body. The mind becomes less
cluttered and thoughts don't intrude.
Emotions aren't felt so strongly.

You are able to disconnect from the
body, mind and emotions and at the
same time become *more* connected
to the whole.

Heartbeat

Focus on the rhythmic beat of your heart.
    Breathe slowly and without effort.
    Silently repeat as a mantra: 'I am calm
now. Nothing else matters.'

Meditate deeply

The quickest way to reach the Alpha
level, where the brainwave patterns are
slower than the normal waking state, is
to use what some people call a 'circular
breath'.

To breathe this way, draw your breath
in down the back of your throat rather
than down the front, which is the normal
way of breathing.

Circles of light

Use circular breathing to wrap your body
in circles or hoops of light, from head to
toe. Draw the circles with your mind's
eye. Place the circles next to and over
each other till you have filled the body,
then lay them on their sides and wrap
them around the width of the body.
Imagine that you are cleansing the
body, ridding it of toxins.

Meditate on a mandala

A mandala is a circle, a symbol of
wholeness. The rose windows in
Christian churches are mandalas.
Mandalas have within them objects
of contemplation (for example,
a cross or a square) or representations
of wholeness or divinity (such as the
Om symbol or the Christ figure).

Meditate on a mandala with your
eyes open.

Past, present and future

Draw a large circle and then a small circle at the centre. Meditate on what you feel is the predominant colour of your name. Fill in the small circle with this colour.

Divide the rest of the circle into your *past, present and future* and meditate on each, before drawing in the spaces.

Pin the mandala on a wall.

Meditation and colour

Every colour is composed of light waves
and has a different vibrational energy.
Some colours are calming and others
are arousing. Mental hospital walls are
painted in soothing colours to influence
the patients' mental state.

Meditating on colour reduces stress.

'Breathing' rainbows

Meditate on the colours of the rainbow
from red to violet. Immerse yourself in
each colour. Breathe it in and feel its
energy. Does it affect some parts of your
body more than others? What emotions
do you feel with each colour? What
thoughts, what memories, surface?

Meditate on the chakras

In some books on meditation you'll find 'chakras' mentioned. The chakras are defined in ancient Indian texts as the spiritual energy centres of the body. Each chakra (root, sacral, solar plexus, heart, throat, brow, crown) has a predominant colour. Each chakra is also associated with certain organs in the body, and with particular mental qualities.

Lotus flowers

Imagine each chakra centre as a lotus
flower that gradually opens its petals.
Begin at the root chakra (red), and
proceed through orange, yellow, green,
blue, indigo, to the crown chakra (violet).
Above the crown chakra, visualise
white light.

Structured meditation

As its name suggests, a structured
meditation has a definite form.
It is more like an exercise to help
you develop your powers of attention,
observation, and concentration.

It disciplines the body and the mind
so that meditation can become easy.

Breath counting

Begin with a relaxed body.
Focus *only* on the breath entering and
leaving the nostrils.
Don't let the mind wander. If it does,
bring it back.
Count to four as you breathe in, and to
four as you breathe out.
Do the breath counting for five minutes.
Reflect on the exercise.

Unstructured meditation

An unstructured meditation is one in
which the activity is not completely
defined. This sort of meditation develops
its own form as you do it. You can never
be sure where an unstructured
meditation will take you. It is exciting,
unpredictable and leads to personality
growth.

Connecting

Imagine a starry sky. Some stars are
especially bright. You notice them.
These stars are the links in your personal
world. Draw each star to you and identify
a person and the special qualities he or
she brings to you. Why do you need
these qualities and what do you give
back in return?

Allow for things to happen.

Meditate on abundance

Life is an adventure when you leave
behind the limitations you set yourself.
Meditation makes you realise that only
fear and negative beliefs stop your 'good'
coming to you.

Recognise and accept opportunities.
Don't let them pass you by.

Vision

In what areas of your life are you lacking?
Choose one and visualise the situation *as
you wish it to be*. Note your feelings and
thoughts in this state of abundance, then
look at what you are doing (believing,
feeling, acting) to sabotage yourself.

Meditation gives you feedback

There are machines that monitor the body and its response to stress. When you meditate, you won't need a machine. You'll become super-aware. You can 'talk' with your body to ask it questions and find the wise person within. The answers come.

The conflict within

Reflect on a difficult situation in your life. Breathe deeply and stay with the associated feelings. Don't let the head take over. Allow thoughts about the conflict to come in. Don't force or impose them.

Converse with whoever comes into your mind picture, whether they are the 'cause' of the conflict, the wise person within, or the child part of yourself.

Meditation is practical

If you thought that meditation is only for monks and monasteries, you're wrong. It's good for adults *and* children. It can be done wherever you are, whether it's a crowded room or your back garden. You can meditate while the world's collapsing around you, or when you are happy.

There is no time, nor place, that *isn't* appropriate for meditation.

Try meditating. . .

- While you are on the toilet
- While doing the job you hate most
- Before an interview
- Sitting on a beach
- In bed
- In a small, enclosed space
- While looking at the clock face

Meditation and perfection

Look around at nature and you'll see
a wonderful state of imperfection; the
gnarled, bent tree growing out of the cliff
face has beauty and character. Perfection
is an artificial perception for which many
of us strive. It has more to do with rigidity
and judgement than high standards.
Meditation will bring growth and
awareness, not perfection.

The way you are

The way you are now is okay. Accept your-self just as you are and know that, over time, you will change. Don't put yourself down, or compare yourself with others. Concentrate on your own uniqueness. Encourage yourself.

Meditation's path of action

It's not necessary to retreat inside yourself, or to be an ascetic, to realise the benefits of meditation.

Some people are happier immersing themselves in action, as did Mother Teresa, who worked with the poor in the slums of Calcutta.

Your path of action is your choice.

A passionate choice

Select an activity or a cause that you feel
strongly about. Give time and energy to
it. Put your heart and soul into it. When
you are involved in it, you will be so *deeply*
involved that nothing else matters. Time
passes without knowing. There is content-
ment and satisfaction.

Meditation and the emotions

Emotions are like shifting sands –
unstable, elusive. It's difficult to know
what you really feel when feelings
change from one day to the next.

Meditation helps you sort out what is
real and what is not – what you are taking
on from other people, and what you are
projecting.

You realise that your emotions,
like your thoughts, are *your* choices.

Emotional labels

Make a list of all the negative emotional
states such as anger, jealousy, hatred,
despair and grief.

What thoughts and wider beliefs are
behind the emotion you have labelled?

Look at the fears and blocks that hold
the emotions in place.

Meditate on the positive

It's so easy to concentrate on the negative in ourselves and in others. Bring back the balance by focusing on what is positive and affirming.

Use affirmations in your meditation. These are positively worded statements that you can repeat, either aloud or silently.

Feel the meaning of your affirmation and eventually you will change the way you think.

Affirmation

Compose an affirmation in the present.
Make sure there are no indirect negatives.
Write the affirmation in as many different
ways as you can.
Carry it in your mind wherever you go.
Use breathing to take you deeper.

Example: 'I am fearless, and free.'

Meditation and the guru

In eastern cultures, it is common for novices in meditation to have a guru or a master who will teach them, maybe for several years. The learning may involve living with the guru in a place called an 'ashram'.

You don't need a guru to learn meditation, but it's likely that you will learn from someone who knows more about it than you.

The hermit

Visualise an old person, full of wisdom
and experience, who lives in a cave in
the mountains. Make a pilgrimage there.
Bring an offering (a gift of your choice)
and sit at the feet of the hermit. Ask for
general guidance, or ask questions about
a specific issue. Listen well and don't
interrupt!

Meditation reduces stress

When you are stressed, everything fails you. You lack energy, become sick more easily, can't think logically, and your feelings run wild. You are in a state of *not* coping.

If you know how to meditate, you can not only handle stress, but also eliminate it from many areas of your life.

Variations on a theme

You can't predict when a stressful situation will happen, so be forewarned: look at the *last* one. Place yourself back in it and observe. What is your predominant emotion or thought? Where did it come from? Who or what are you blaming or justifying? Look for patterns in the things that happen to you. How will you behave differently the next time? Mentally rehearse.

Meditation clues

Relax the body first.
Practise deep breathing.
It's easier for most people to fill the mind
rather than empty it, so start with
concentration and visualisation.
Meditate in the same place each time:
it helps you develop a habit.
Develop one ritual that you always adopt
when you meditate.

Some books to begin with

Greer Allica *Meditation Workbook*
Shakti Gawain *Creative Visualization*
Lawrence LeShan *How to Meditate*
Paul Wilson *The Calm Technique*

Meditation and discrimination

Being able to say: 'This is good for me'
or 'This is a destructive force in my life'
is empowering. Meditation helps you
know the difference. You can make these
decisions without condemning yourself
or others.

The wisdom within

Knowing what is good for you depends
on being able to say no, recognising what
is yours and what belongs to others (on
all levels), being kind to yourself,
eliminating confusion by having a clear
focus, understanding your needs.

Reach for the wisdom inside you by
connecting to the wisdom of the universe.

Meditation is release

Nothing in your life can change unless
you let go of something already there
that is hindering your progress. Decay,
death and birth are part of the process
of change. Inner release mirrors outer
release, so get rid of something in
your physical world.

The clearing house

Visualise a house. Walk inside and go
through each room, collecting the
rubbish you find. Load it onto the truck
waiting outside and drive to the clearing
house. Unload the rubbish and look at
what is there. Mentally release it from
your life.

Return to your tidy house. What are
you feeling?

Meditation connects

You see similarities rather than differences.
You understand how personal conflict
mirrors group conflict.
You connect what you do with what
you think.
You feel a link with the world of nature.

Making a difference

Pick one of the points on the opposite page and meditate on it. How can you contribute to a better world? It doesn't have to be mind-shattering. Take a positive step forward – either small or big.

Meditate on the child within

It's easy to forget that everyone (even you!) has a child within. The 'child' is spontaneous, curious, full of joy and wonder. The child is also *naturally* trusting. These qualities are already within you.

Of course, there is also the hurt child, the fearful or dependent child, the child who has temper tantrums.

Another way of seeing

If you could look at your life through
the eyes of a child, using a child's positive
perception, how would you see things?
Which childlike quality would you like
to have more of? Make it happen.

Meditate on the good in your life

It's so easy to take for granted all that you have. Appreciate your own qualities. Mentally thank the people (those who are living, and those who have gone before you), who have shared their knowledge and given support. Look at your physical surroundings and give thanks for the shelter that you have, for the natural beauty around you. Be aware of the contributions of the wider community.

Reaching out

- Write a letter or card, or telephone a special person in your life. Let them know how and why you appreciate them.
- Give a small gift to someone you love.
- Hold a party to thank your friends.
- Make some practical contribution to your community.
- Give away one of your precious possessions.

Meditation is *conscious* living

Once you can meditate, you'll know where you are going. You won't feel at the mercy of life. At the same time, you'll be open to the 'flow' and won't try to control everything. To live consciously is to live knowingly, so that every moment matters. Your life becomes a jewel of your own crafting.

The whole picture

To get an idea of the patterns in your life,
draw a number of circles on a page. Start
with the beginning of your life and move
towards the present. Inside each circle
name (in a few words) an experience
that has helped shape your life.

What links can you see between the
circles?

Meditation brings clarity

Meditation is like using a highlighter pen
on a page of writing: it draws into focus
all that is significant. The writing is your
imprint on the world – what you do
and say. Without order and focus,
nothing is clear.

Inner seeing

Think of an issue that disturbs you.
Imagine you are in a dark forest. In the
depths of the forest you come to a deep
pool, surrounded by small pebbles. As
you throw the pebbles into the water,
throw in your problem. Notice the
expanding ripples. Watch them as they
deepen and then see the surface become
clear and still.

Meditate often

If you want meditation to be easy, you
need to do it often. By doing it regularly,
you'll get used to it. You'll find your own
blocks faster – physical distraction,
inability to visualise, not making time,
or whatever. Meditating often, gives
meditation priority in your life.

Blocks

What is stopping you meditating?
What is stopping you doing it regularly, or enjoying it? Look deeply inside yourself.

If you don't make time to meditate, ask yourself these questions:

What is my pay-off?

Do I deserve time for myself?

Are my needs as important as other people's?

Do I believe that meditation will help me?

Meditation and the mind

Meditation teaches you how to control
your mind so that it doesn't control you.
Before anything can become manifest,
there must be a thought. Through
meditation you'll learn to strengthen,
clarify, sort, examine and release
your thoughts.

The tree of knowledge

Connect to the universal mind. Imagine yourself as a tree. Through your feet, feel grounded. Know that you are nourished through your roots by the earth beneath.

From your head and your arms, imagine branches that reach out to the sky and are fed by the air and the sun.

Meditation is . . . *easy*

Meditation never *was* difficult, though
it's developed that reputation. It's not
intellectual or esoteric, nor is it necessarily
spiritual. Anyone can learn it *if he or she
really wants to*, and that is the only
qualifier – are you motivated enough?

Unravelling a ball of wool

If you let a ball of wool become
unravelled, it ends up a knotted mess,
but if you wind it onto a piece of card,
there are no problems.

It is just so with meditation – it can be
difficult if you go about it the wrong way
and with preconceived ideas. Find a
system that suits you, and a structure.
Your way of learning is not the same as
the next person's.